GW01157953

Martin Newell is a writer and m
rock bands, he came out of the
published in *The Guardian* in 198
poems and features for *The Indep*
taking up his current posts as
Express and columnist for the *East Anglian Daily Times*. He's
previously published a dozen collections of verse, two social
histories a collection of his columns and a memoir of his glam
rock days. He divides his time between the late Regency period
and the present day. He lives in Essex.

The Wife of '55

Martin Newell

Nasty Little Press

Published by Nasty Little Press in September 2013.

Nasty Little Press
35 St Johns Road, Bungay, Suffolk, NR35 1DH
nastylittlepress.org | @nastylit

ISBN: 978-0-9573000-7-1

A CIP record of this book is available from the British Library.

Set in Book Antiqua.

Printed and bound by Berforts Information Press Ltd.

Cover illustration by Hilary Lazell.

Dedicated to Beryl - my mum!

Contents

THE WIFE OF '55

The Wife of '55

History forgets her now
the wife of 'Fifty-five
the tea upon the table
she'd struggle to contrive
a plate of bread and butter
some pilchards or some Spam
they asked if she was happy
she'd sigh and say "I am."

A woman's work, they told her
the totems said it all
the copper-stick, the mangle
a clothes-horse in the hall
the polish and the soda
a bunker for the coal
a wireless for the soundtrack
the garden for her soul.

"Waste bread, you'll live to want it."
her mother used to say
the Sunday joint, the dripping
she'd use another day
the bones for broth or stockpot
the scraps for dog or birds
it wasn't called recycling
or other fancy words.

A perm on Friday evening
some powder on her face
when Saturday was tipsy
and husband might give chase
a comma in her sentence
when time itself stood still
if history forgets her
the children never will.

The Morning Train

The Hythe has had a shower today
sluiced the weary night away
the platform, wet from recent rain
is standing for the London train.
In sight of automatic gates
the backbone of the nation waits
the clouds are hanging out to dry
for soon the sun will scale the sky.

With gelled-up hair, the younger chaps
and too much aftershave, perhaps
in crumpled jackets, scruffy shoes
go late to jobs, they'd hate to lose.
Yawning then, they find a place
to hide themselves in cyber-space
sequestered in a comfort zone
of laptop, iPod, mobile phone.

Somewhere near to Seven Kings
a salesgirl thinks engagement rings
drains her polystyrene cup
and then, reluctantly, moves up
recalling waterfront estates
in seats not made for vertebrates
for in the hour or so it takes
the backbone of the nation aches.

The Evening Train

Past Ingatestone the wheels complain
a whine of brakes, the evening train
has stopped in woods beside the line
autumnal now but clear and fine.
With heaters ticking under seats
the sleepers dream suburban streets
pints of beer and pubs and home
on mattresses of memory foam .

Near end of week, within an hour
at Colchester, the water tower
informs them that they're almost back
with coats already off the rack
impatient in the aisles, they'll wait
the backbone of the nation, late
yet grateful for such welcome sights
as partners, buses, taxi lights.

And those few travellers left behind
can all stretch out and never mind
the last few empty miles somehow
the horse can smell the stable now
and farther up the Colne somewhere
a whiff of dampness in the air
reminds them vaguely, on the way
The Hythe has had a shower today.

The Blackberries

When blackberries are ready
they hang in heavy sprays
as clouds pile up the laundry
the pillows, sheets and stays
of summer's dwindled days.
And on the dewy footpaths
by spider webs that slacken
the blackberries will redden
against the rusting bracken
and ripen till they blacken.

It's here the country kitchen
did battle each September
for jam in mid-October
and wine by late December
or fought for thorny hours
got caught in autumn showers
and quietly effed and blinded
but never really minded.

Today, on hills and downland
are laden lanes and ledges
fat with fruit and berries
unpicked across the hedges
that straggle on their edges.
Forgotten for the present

now visited by few
the souls of men are fidgets
they've better things to do
than stain or prick their digits
and hold containers steady
but blackberries are ready
blackberries are ready.

Past Michaelmas

Past Michaelmas the sun is paler
rising like a shore-leave sailor
waking up the groggy day
with October on the way.
Western gales as chamber maids
plumping up the clouds for pillows
bending poplars, shuffling willows.

Geese well-fattened on the stubble
and the loaves, long in the tin.
with the weather now in trouble
but the harvest safely in.

Then the Goose Fair, late September
'Barley-month' its Saxon name
Michaelmas was Quarter Day
when delicious autumn came.
Bird on table, hay in stable
pigs and pannage in the wood
bread and bannock in the bakehouse
larder full and household good.

Our Native Rose

A woman of a certain age
as British in her looks
as brollies in a hallway
a pile of gardening books
a dog-lead on a bannister
a crossword on a chair
a kirby grip or headscarf
to hold her honey hair.
A modicum of make up
her unpretentious air
she'll be aware of fashion
though, possibly, won't care
and looks as good off-duty
when standing with a chap
as presidential beauty
who's done up in full-slap

But don't you think she's lovely
in autumn, after rain
walking in a westerly
along some rural lane?
Her battered waxy jacket
chelsea boots and jeans
better than a dozen
of your bony catwalk queens.
For a pale rose complexion
and a seascape in her eyes
for the landscape of her figure

whatever shape or size
for the humour in expression
and the cadence of her voice
you wouldn't take a minute
if you had to make a choice.

Ancient Lights

By ruined Roman brickwork
in cold October air
past Michaelmas, on Beryfield
they held St Dennis Fair.
Now damsels dance down Queen St
and meet their modern knights
while trains come into Colchester
beneath these ancient lights.

On early Norman arches
the blue-eyed jackdaws perch
above those cloistered shadows
behind the Gothic church.
A greensward for their carpet
they gaze down from the heights
for alms the tourists leave them
beneath these ancient lights

Below St Botolph's Circus
across the traffic's roar
the souls of nameless soldiers
go back and forth to war.
In court each winter morning
the sun reads out his rights
the prisoner stands there, yawning
and longs for ancient lights.

While medieval rooftops
stare up at steel and glass
the past reminds the future
to let the present pass
when August flirts with autumn
and starry are the nights
and Colchester lies twinkling
among the ancient lights.

The Lodger

The wardrobe Edwardian, varnished and dark
a bedstead, an eiderdown, out of the ark

the loo on the landing, a geyser, a heater
bathnight on Friday, a bob for the meter

the paint-upon-paint, and the cat in the hall
but always a homeliness over it all.

She had a spare room, we needed the tin
the bed was made up and a lodger moved in.

He worked in a factory, had his own car,
took to the family, called your mum 'Ma'.

We needed the money, it wasn't a case
of wittering on about 'personal space.'

He sang in a tenor, could carry a tune
he went home to Wales, once a blue moon.

It was maybe less private to take in these men
yet, there wasn't a National Loneliness then.

Mrs. Wright's Waste-Food Policy

The blue-tits liked the bacon rind
the sparrows ate the crusts of bread
and anything the cat refused
the dog would often eat instead.
Even tiny crumbs were saved
the tablecloth being gathered up
and shaken on the kitchen lawn
in times before fast-food was born.
"Throw bread upon the fire," she'd say,
"you'll live to want it, come one day."

We never wasted food back then
or not that I recall as such
the leftovers, such as we'd got
were fried and seasoned, served up hot
as rissoles, maybe once a week
or mashed in bubble & squeak.
Firm Edwardian economics
founded Gran's domestic laws
thrift the motto and its cause
sharpened over two world wars.

You never threw the stuff away
for this would be the greatest sin
and what she'd scrape into a bin
would hardly fill a baked bean tin.

But had she lived to learn about
the food-waste bins which Whitehall planned
oh, she'd approve, of course she would.
It's just, she wouldn't understand.

To HP Sauce

A sauce of pleasure – and of salt
of vinegar, of dates, of malt
of sugar, spices, tamarinds
brought in by ships on temperate winds
from warmer climes in which they'd grown
than those our native ports had known
then cooked into a spicy brew
this sauce, this elixir, this goo
decanted, set upon the table
fluted bottle, pale blue label.

Poured on steaks and watery spuds
to cut through cold-clogged, smoke-fugged buds
in foggy weeks on smoggy days
in roadside restaurants and cafes
and placed on pukka larder shelves
by order of the Lords themselves.
For chips and chops, the last anointment
naturally it's by appointment:
commoner and king endorse
the zing. Arise, Sir HP Sauce.

Old WAGs

They dwelt in semis, quietly then
read *Woman's Own* and *Woman's Realm*
cooked shepherd's pie, bubble & squeak
and had their hair done once a week
more Marks' n 'Sparks than French boutique.

The wives and girls of players then
were unaccustomed to the light
no Vuitton bags or Jimmy Choos
the public never saw their shoes
or even knew whose wives were whose.

Those *quietly pretty* hometown girls
were not the stuff of tabloids then
they rarely jetted to the States
were snapped in gardens, stood by gates
Did not eye up their husbands' mates
Unemancipated, clearly.
You wonder how they managed, really.

The Clocks Go Back

The oaks are brassy golden
the sun's a pat of butter
autumn feeds the brazier
while winter does the shutter
there's coal smoke on the terrace
and summer's in the gutter.

And every starling's in the sky
late in orange afternoon
when clouds
are western wagon trains
and geese are skeins
across the moon.
Parliaments that reconvene
down the days to Halloween.

The sunset hits the fanlight
illuminates the hall
paints a pale rainbow
by the coat-pegs on the wall.
And with October nearly gone
the kettle and the lights go on
in bronchial streets where buses cough
Nature lays the workers off.

Somewhere in a country town
the year, the old year's
running down
whatever shadows it has cast
the bulk of it
has sidled past
Doused its fire and shouldered pack
the clocks, the clocks are
going back.

The Job of Unemployment

It's heavy daytime telly
or a shuffle round the block
while clumsy seconds clatter
through the hands upon the clock
The days stubbed out like dog-ends
the minutes poured like tea
in the job of unemployment
for a job it seems to me.

And the workers who must do it
have their work cut out for sure
in the skips of leaden hours
trundled daily through the door
while days merge into lifetimes
the seasons drift and turn
and stokers man the furnaces
for those with time to burn.

Who never knew a Friday
with a packet to collect
or how the notes and coins
give a thrill of self-respect
when entering a pub, a shop
to gesture at a shelf
for items which you pay for
in money earned yourself.

Now, some say work is slavery
and never makes you free
but the job of unemployment
seems the hardest one to me.

Dad Dancing

Please don't dance, Dad!
Please don't dance!
Spare us any *yeah yeah yeahs*
flapping by in vintage flares
lost in your nostalgic trance.
This we utter in our prayers:
"Please don't dance, Dad!
Never dance."

When a *Six-Ts Nite* spins by
on the dance floor after beer
snapping fingers, shouting "Gear!"
to the hits of yesteryear
paisley shirt and kipper tie
don't dance, Dad
don't even try.

Though Watusi, Twist and Frug
were the dances you once 'dug'
only you remember them
please think twice,
you'll ruin the rug.

Dancing like an egg on legs
or a badly-loaded sack
While your worried family begs:
"Stop, before you do your back."

Spare your sacroiliac!
Please don't dance, Dad!
Please.

Don't.

Dance.

The War Memorial

In slate November
post and chain
the paper poppies in the rain
run red beneath a pitted cross
denoting loss.
Eleven chimes
to mark the hour
the jackdaws start, depart the tower
beneath a sky of muted grey
the ragwash day.

And while the wind
which stirs the trees
disturbs a few remaining leaves
the ceremony in the square
is silent there
except a single-engine plane
muffled by the drizzly rain
in echoes to respectful stone
a distant drone.

The football field
suspends its play
the ball's allowed to roll away
the ref will whistle, raise his hand
the players stand
remembering players

now unknown.
The scores recalled in brass and stone.
Or found in furrows
flecked with bone.

Spurgeon Street

On a cobalt winter morning
when the River Colne was high
while the cars across the causeway
went chariot-racing by
with the sunlight as a sniper
and the frosty fields the kill
I wheeled a bike up Spurgeon Street
and stood on Timber Hill.

And Spurgeon Street looked holy
as I gazed down from there
at icing-sugar rooftops
in cold December air
at the downpipes and the gutters
and shapes carved in the shutters
in the shadow of St Leonard's
with its pinnacles and tower
and I could have stayed an hour
I could have stayed an hour.

In the quietness of the side streets
in their alternating light
with cats asleep in windows
and people out of sight
in the whistle of the kettles
and the tinkle of their spoons
the secrets of the English
are known to churchyard moons

the picture frames on dressers
their private madeleines
and I gaze back at Spurgeon Street
and all that it retains.

The Winter

After western gales have done
heaved the grey autumnal seas
weakened an anaemic sun
anaesthetised the bees
drained the sap from all the trees
substituted golds for greens
covered summer's murder scenes
with a distant roll of drums
winter comes, winter comes.

Like a surgeon to his rounds
down a chilly corridor
taciturn, he beats the bounds
squeaky shoes upon the floor
murmuring behind each screen
while the patient pale in bed
strains to overhear what's said
firmly then, but without fuss
winter enters thus.

When the slate is clean at dawn
and at first, the frost seems light
steaming off each sunlit lawn
like a mistress taking flight
from a chamber not yet hers
now the night draws in so early
and the north-east wind is surly
as the mask begins to slip
winter cracks its whip.

Down the ginnels winter slips
into country towns it knows
paperboys blow fingertips
stood on doorsteps, freezing toes
kicking empty bottles over
setting yappy terriers off
then the cancerous buses cough
and it rains in panel pins
so a winter day begins

Under downlands to the south
where the chalkhill horses sleep
trains speed from a tunnel mouth
scattering crows and shaking sheep
on the windy downs, the dewponds
high above the Pilgrims Way
keep their icy glaze all day
neolithic farmers knew them;
winter's wading through them.

Whistling near a lonely bandstand
starching leafmould in the park
greeting in an empty grandstand
spectral sportsmen in the dark
but the boating pond is frozen
and the punts are put away
for some far-off summer day
in the brown and broken nettles
winter settles, winter settles.

Yet, it makes its reparations
in the rose-gold frosty air
smoky applewood for perfume
worn as if for some affair
mulled in inglenooks with liquor
dalliances suit the season.
Need we look for any reason
huddled by a crackling fire?
Winter kindles such desire.

Even the imperious City
peers out at the falling snow
while alarms shriek out a ditty
to deserted streets below:
"Wi-wi-wi-wi-we are waiting.
with our wilted mistletoe
seasonal trading has been slow
will no one invest in kisses?
What a waste of money this is."

But the cabs will still be queueing
passing Oxford Street's fantasia
and the chestnuts will be doing
in nostalgia's golden brazier.
Time re-screens the past in sepia
for the wistful eyes of men
did we not keep Christmas then
better, in our long-lost youth?
Only winter knows that truth.

Christmas of the past was cosy
we forget the days more fraught
in the pub the world looks rosy
filtered through a glass of port
red as berries on the holly
it's the spirit we recall.
Christmas in the Baron's Hall
loud with stories and charades
winter lives on Christmas cards.

Coaching inns and horns hallooing
horses, hounds, a stovepipe hat
parcels, puddings, Bishop brewing
was a Christmas ever that?
Crone in rags, her faggot bundle
struggling in a snowy lane
here such icons will remain
hung in halls of old Decembers
visions dancing in the embers.

How will winter wear its beauty?
like the widow of an earl
elegantly at her duty
pale as a grieving girl
as the snowflakes fall at midnight
cold confetti on her head
ah, the year, the old year's dead
underneath its snowy bier
fields and farmland disappear.

Sleep delicious, sleep profound
swansdown swathes the woodland floor
summer's somewhere underground
sleeping depths un-plumbed before.
While the spring remains in exile
like a prince, long overseas
not a whisper of a breeze
nor a captain at the helm
can return him to his realm.

Daylight breaks on snowfall steady.
silent swirling swarms of bees
hide the huntsman, horse at ready
waiting in a copse of trees.
Flushed from cover comes the quarry
muted horn, a creature calling
trampled snow, the body falling
winter goes in for the kill
now the conquered land is still.

How does winter end its reign?
Like a guest who stays and stays
leaves but then returns again
without notice – and for days.
Grudgingly, curmudgeonly,
in a harsh persistent wind
chillblained feet and broken-skinned
influenza on his breath
winter dies a drawn-out death

But the earth will wake, the hedges
turn to luminescent green
wildfowl jostles in the sedges
while a buttery sun is seen
warming up the frosty furrows
watched in rolling early mist
brandishing a bony fist
winter glowers vainly back
melting on the muddy track.

Threadneedle Street

Old Lady of Threadneedle Street
in your impassive stone
a monument to mammon
in the rumble and the drone
of ceaseless City traffic
you sat there on your own
from thirsty dusty summers
to pinching winter days
while pigeons fluffed and bickered
or mated in your bays.

With clouds of war above you
and the wealth of England under
still they'd mill around you
like rats in your rotunda
who seldom saw the sun shine
and hardly heard the thunder
while gathered round their abacuses
did they ever wonder

what hats had passed your portals?
whose tricorns and cockades?
whose stovepipes and whose bowlers
had known your colonnades?
Or felt the endless footfall
across your well-worn stone
inscrutable Old Lady
silent and alone.

A House on The Hill

Up there among the gouts of cloud
above the teeming hoi polloi
the agent said we should be proud
she warranted that we'd enjoy
a prospect of the distant Park
its tracer bullet queues of cars
returning in the winter dark
to gated Heights with window bars.

We padded round our belvedere
which overlooked less-classy Ways
the common Roads and Terraces
we'd camped in, during younger days.
In claustrophobic Courts we'd waited
Closes cramped, devoid of views
till gradually, we graduated
gratefully to Avenues.

We travelled ever upwards then,
through leafy Lanes and cobbled Mews
yet, nothing could be perfect till
we'd joined those folks upon the Hill.

Angry Young Men
(dedicated to Alan Sillitoe)

From a country grey with tiredness
in the dust of settled wars
in the cabbage-scented hallways
with brown linoleum floors
came a clattering of writers
behind the terraced doors
of young men home from service
now ravenous for choice
who smoked and drank for England
while struggling for their voice.

Over black and rainy rooftops
over bombsites left to flowers
in the offices and bookshops
for interminable hours
they would paint accusing pictures:
polemic, prose and rhyme
being young before the Sixties
yet, old before their time.
While paperbacks in millions
would fill the nation's shelves
until, too soon, the young men
had all grown old themselves.

Children's Ward 1950s

She'd sat up at her desk all night
a kindly, reassuring shape
her shift now done,
she donned her cape
eloping quietly at first light
with darkness, like a bride,
a powdery April snow had fallen
dusting roofs outside.
A tiny patient gave a cough
and all the shadows tiptoed off.

In caps and aprons stiff with starch
the morning shift marched in
through corridors so clean they'd squeak
scented for the working week
with isopropanol, which masked
the flowers on polished tables
"Has it snowed?" a child asked.

"A little, yes," the sister said
and turned the wireless on for him
poured him out some watery squash
placed a headset on his head
straightened the wheels on his bed
checked her fob-watch, pulled a cord
and let the sun into the ward.

Brief Encounter Revisited

Heppy? I suppose I was...
until that fateful day
our lovely station tea room
became a chain cafe.
For hed we shared some scones perheps,
a bar of fruit and nut
it might have saved our
doomed affair.
However, they were shut.

An ordinary housewife
and doctor, met by chance
your ticket, then, was Anytime
and mine a Cheap Advance.
Being subject to the National Rails
Conditions of Carriage
our love was non-transferable
ruling out a merriage.

Hed we met on Sundays
I might have worn a het
weekend engineering works
put a stop to thet.
Love could never flourish
or not, at least, for us
rumbling down a motorway
in some replacement bus.

No wonder you decided then
not to tie the knot
and took thet job in Efrica.
Heppy? No I'm not.

Dentist Drill

There is a house, a sombre house
on each Victorian avenue
beside the darkling laurel trees
where dentists do the work they do.
Only a tattered *Country Life*
to whittle anxious minutes through
distracts the mind from whining drills
not quite disguised by Radio Two.

And now, your name is called
as here, the chamber waits
the bib, the chair
the visor and the suction pipe
the dentist and assistant there.
For buccal or occlusal fills
they'll need to use those dreadful drills.
Soon the mining will begin
as if your teeth were coal or tin.

And seemingly, a day may pass
until he puts amalgam in
your hands clutched tight
you lie and wince
and pray to hear the words
"Now rinse."
Then, Quasimodo-faced and grim.
you exit, dimly, thanking him.

In Flaming June...

Within that sodden woodland
a summer in disgrace
as elderflower bunches weep
upon the Queen Anne's Lace
the rain it drums for England
the season's out of tune
the moon's a tarnished ingot
the sun's a dull doubloon
skulking under duvets
of thick unlaundered cloud
soaked for days, the squirrel dreys
in hawthorn trees are bowed
and yet, the birdsong's loud.

It echoes at each dawning
on streets estranged from dust
umbrellas meet in mourning
their struts now stained by rust.
On wet suburban station roads
from Hounslow, east to Epping
broadbrim-hat commuters watch
in overcoats still dripping
partners dragging dogs home
on sodden latticed bridges
to curse as creatures shake their pelts
near pristine kitchen fridges.

The country has surrendered
resistance being in vain
poor vanquished sun,
the battle won
by ruthless General Rain.

An Essex Girl

An Essex girl - an 'Essex calf'
she'll never mind it
if you laugh
or substitute bad jokes for wit
she's heard them all
she's used to it
she'll note the things you say and do
before she stops to yawn at you.

Her native style
her smoke-blue eyes
underlined in pencil black
were sharpened under endless skies
where linseed flowers
and poppies grow
in summer fields laid out below.

And if her mode of speech
seems plain
don't underestimate, again,
her power to say what she may think
once she's matched you
drink for drink
grabbed her bag and paid the tab
mentioned work
and called a cab.
Lawyer, lecturer, actress, nurse.
An Essex girl?
You could do worse.

The Suffolk Punch

I met a horse the other day
a Suffolk Sorrel
ches'nut brown
the wind sliced in off
Hollesley Bay
as in its wake
the rain came down

And all the while the horse
stood still
underneath an ancient oak
inscrutable, as if I were
the butt of some old equine joke
which all the horses over years
had told each other –
but not me

And there we were, the two of us
man and horse by dripping tree.
A rainy summer's afternoon
one Saturday – a country fete
standard fare for middle June
an April shower – turned up late.

At last the Suffolk Punch
turned round,
acknowledging that it was wet.

He shook his mane
and pawed the ground
snorting at me once,
"Well met."

The Last Postcard

Scribbled in a candlewickian
bedroom of a B&B
purchased back in sunny Clacton
August, nineteen sixty-three
on a garish golden morning
with a ninety-five watt sun
saucy seaside postcard planets
light years from our present one.

Here the drunks with cherry noses
shrug and hiccup at their spouses
overblown old British roses
beachball bottoms, big as houses;
goggle-eyed, pneumatic nurses
in their overshortened skirts
having bandaged some appendage
ask the patient if it hurts.

Till the final postcard's posted
scrawled and sent with love and kisses,
Blimey, strewth and *ooh-er missus*
doctors, tarts, salacious vicars
fade into the blue horizon
in a rain of bras and knickers.

The New Tourists

They'd known the River Nile
yet not the River Naddle
they'd flown the world in style
and never been to paddle
the North Sea near to Frinton
or Cornish Riviera
but went to California
to hike the High Sierra.

They'd wandered over Umbria
seen Trasimeno's shores
yet never been to Cumbria
or tramped the Yorkshire Moors.
They'd toured the Wall of China
but not the tors of Devon
cruised the world by liner
yet never seen the Severn.

With price of flights expensive
and myriad complications
they'd grown more apprehensive
of earlier destinations
so trains and cars and campers
were ways employed to go
to tour the only country
they'd never got to know.

Abroad and all its treasures
they'd substitute this year
for simpler earthy pleasures
a ploughman's and a beer.
Nice, if nothing fancy
with sandwiches to nibble
for folk who'd seen the Yangtze
but not the River Ribble.

Spring and Port Lane

Let me see you home again
in the hat-pins of the rain
Timber Hill and Parsons Lane
Up Hythe Hill in heartbeats.

This romance conducted here
after chips and pints of beer
till we overcome our fear
Up Hythe Hill in heartbeats.

Up the road to Jan & Phil's
major cures for minor ills
I will bring your headache pills
Up Hythe Hill in heartbeats.

In the traffic of the day
Greenstead Road to Lightship Way
can I stop the cars to say
that we are now an item?

Like two cygnets in the sedge
moorhens on the water's edge
all along these banks I pledge
love ad infinitum.

48

Ernie Doe's to B&Qs
hammered out in four-be-twos
tell the whole wide world the news
I will still adore you.

Till the lorries cease to rumble
till the sales run out of jumble
till the Uni towers crumble
I will tumble 4 U.

Up Hythe Hill and home again
past the rainbow on Port Lane
hung there like a petrol stain
Up Hythe Hill in heartbeats.

Walk with ghosts of engineers
fishermen and cavaliers
through the cavalcade of years
Up Hythe Hill in heartbeats .

Up Hythe Hill in soaking jeans
wind in trees, like tambourines
only we know what this means
only we know what this means
only we know what this means
Up Hythe Hill in heartbeats.

The Coming of The Railways

When the railway navvies came
all the countryside awoke
to the yells of men and gangers
dragging wagons, spikes and iron
in a fog of pitch and smoke.

They dug with picks and shovels
into ballast and to clay
they scored across the surfaces
of sleeping fields and slopes
and began to make their way.

Like a vast and godless army
raised of dark industrial pride
with the stamina of oxen
they tore into their labour
fought and often died.

Made huts from turf and pit-props
in the damp and stinking mud
where they bedded down, exhausted
at the end of nameless days
only sinew, bone and blood.

Here they'd pull the houses down
and there, they'd level land
the timbermen and tippers
the spannermen and nippers

for this had all been planned.

And nothing now could stop them
while the future beat its drum
and a fever took the nation
through the blood of speculation
when the railway had to come.

They camped beside embankments
by the cuttings and the drains
the English, Scots and Irishmen
brutalised and maddened
for the sake of running trains.

Now, wagons came to serve them
with the whisky and the beer
the grocers with provisions
the tommy-shops with bait
the locals lived in fear.

For woe betide those villages
or towns when they were paid
it was batten down the hatches
and arm the clerks and servants
and lock away the maid.

As the navvy knew no reason
and he recognised no law
running riot through the parish
till militia men were called
to fell him to the floor.

His life was cheap and wretched
and his home was where he dropped
for his drunken isolation
was the only thing he knew
till his work or heart had stopped.

So, when you ride these rails
know that every yard of land
every cutting and embankment
between London and the sea
was hacked out by his hand.

By a navvy with a shovel
who was caked in muck and mud
in a land of hope and glory
his monument, his story
was sinew, bone and blood.

Well Done, You

Oh, hello and how are *you*?
What is it you say you do?
Writer *and* musician too?
Well done, you!

Both our boys were keen on pop
one of them was in a band
so I know it's very hard
He was at The Juilliard.
And he helped arrange some strings
for a quite good friend of Sting's.
Now he's doing jazz and blues
have *you* ever played a cruise?
Not the type of thing you do?
Still...well done, *you*!

Ah, you have a record out?
Anything I might have heard?
And you made it by yourself?
Oh, you *play* as well as sing
Oooh, you *are* a clever thing!
But you say, it's not quite pop
could I buy it in a shop?
Amazon will stock it too?
Oh, well done, you!

Well done you! Well done *you*!
Our sister's lawyer's cousin's friend

went on holiday last year
skiing in Vermont – or near
she telephoned us, quite amazed
someone there had *heard* of you!
It was absolutely true,
well done, *you*!

How's your little book been doing?
And how's your little record done?
We're aware you worked *quite* hard
still, I bet it's been such fun!
Years ago, when you were young
trying to get on that first rung
many said you never would
though, there were still one or two
who believed – *I* always knew
that you'd make it – Well done, *you*!

How's your little mortgage going?
Forty grand goes nowhere now
but you scraped it up somehow
and you've *got* your working space
so important, don't you think?
Somewhere for your pens and ink
we were mentioning you, in fact
round at dinner, Wednesday night
Christine said, despite it all
underneath, you were quite bright
and you'd *stuck* at what you do
So important. Well done *you*!

Everyone invited there
all remarked how *well* you'd done
with your television piece
though, I never saw that one.
"Big fish in a little pond,"
someone at the table said
even though it might be true
well done, you, well done *you*!

Well done you, well done you
for keeping going, all these years
you deserve success. You *do*!
How d'you think of your ideas?
But why's it you and why not me?
I, at least, got my degree
I could write like you, I bet.
Though, I've not quite started yet.
But your records are a din
I was trained at violin
I should know about such things.
Still – good luck in all you do
Well done, you. Well done *you*!
WELL DONE *YOU*!
WELL DONE *YOU*!

Acknowledgments

I would like to thank Express Newspapers who first published many of these poems. In particular, thanks are due to *Sunday Express* editor Martin Townsend, who often commissions poems from me which almost seem to write themselves. They are among my best work.

I would also thank Colchester Borough Council who commissioned some of the selections herein – initially for the 9.03 Hythe Station project in 2009.

Thanks are due to Young Luke Wright and Nasty Little Press who helped to talk me down and bring this book in for landing. I also thank Ms Hilary Lazell for putting up with me.

As for anyone whom I've omitted, all I can say is, "Well done, you!"